LUST, CAUTION | MUSIC FROM THE MOTION PICTURE SOUNDTRACK | PIANO SOLO

MUSIC BY ALEXANDRE DESPLAT

ISBN 978-1-4234-3620-1

HAL•LEONARD®
CORPORATION
7777 W. BLUEMOUND RD. P.O. BOX 13819 MILWAUKEE, WI 53213

Visit Hal Leonard Online at
www.halleonard.com

LUST, CAUTION

By ALEXANDRE DESPLAT

Very slowly, mysteriously

DINNER WALTZ

By ALEXANDRE DESPLAT

Moderately slow

mp legato

With pedal

8vb

FALLING RAIN

By ALEXANDRE DESPLAT

Moderately

p

With pedal

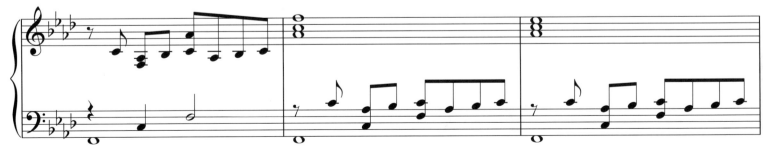

* *Recorded a half step higher.*

BRAHMS INTERMEZZO IN A MAJOR
Op. 118 No. 2

By JOHANNES BRAHMS
Arranged by ALEXANDRE DESPLAT

STREETS OF SHANGHAI

By ALEXANDRE DESPLAT

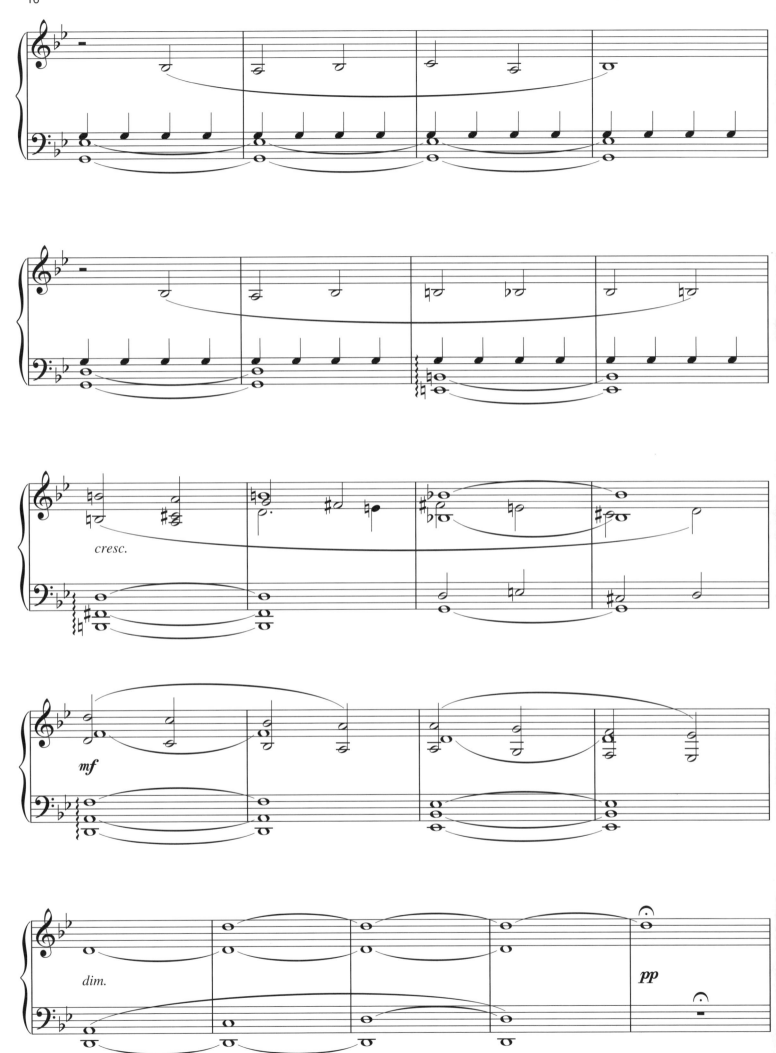

PLAYACTING

By ALEXANDRE DESPLAT

Moderately slow

With pedal

TSIM SHA TSUI STROLL

By ALEXANDRE DESPLAT

Moderately slow, delicately

EXODUS

By ALEXANDRE DESPLAT

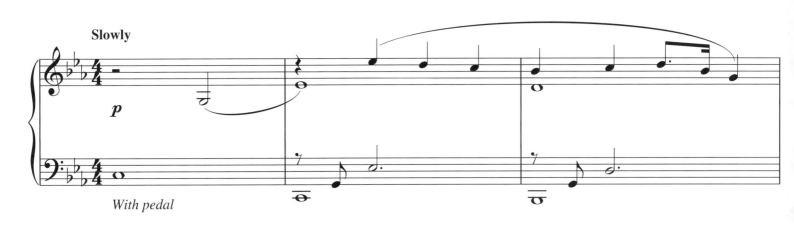

Slowly

p

With pedal

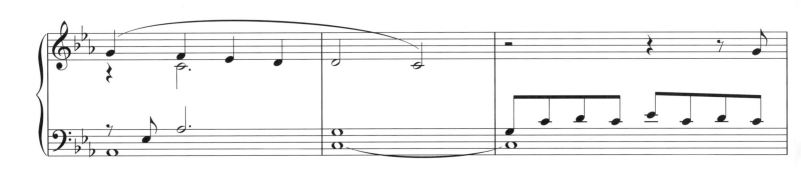

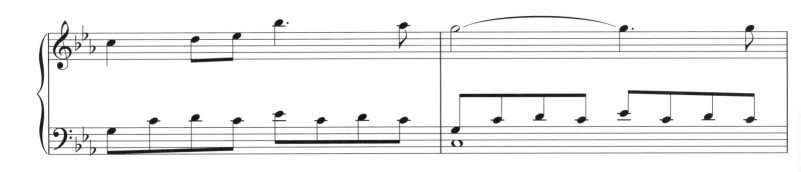

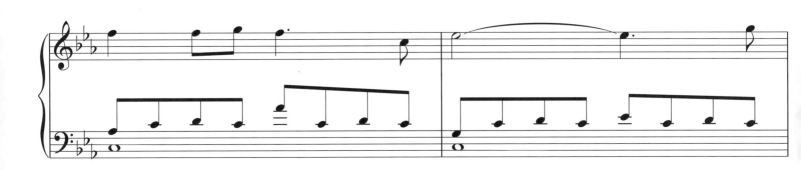

MOONLIGHT DRIVE

By ALEXANDRE DESPLAT

Very slowly

SHANGHAI 1942

By ALEXANDRE DESPLAT

THE END OF INNOCENCE

By ALEXANDRE DESPLAT

With more motion

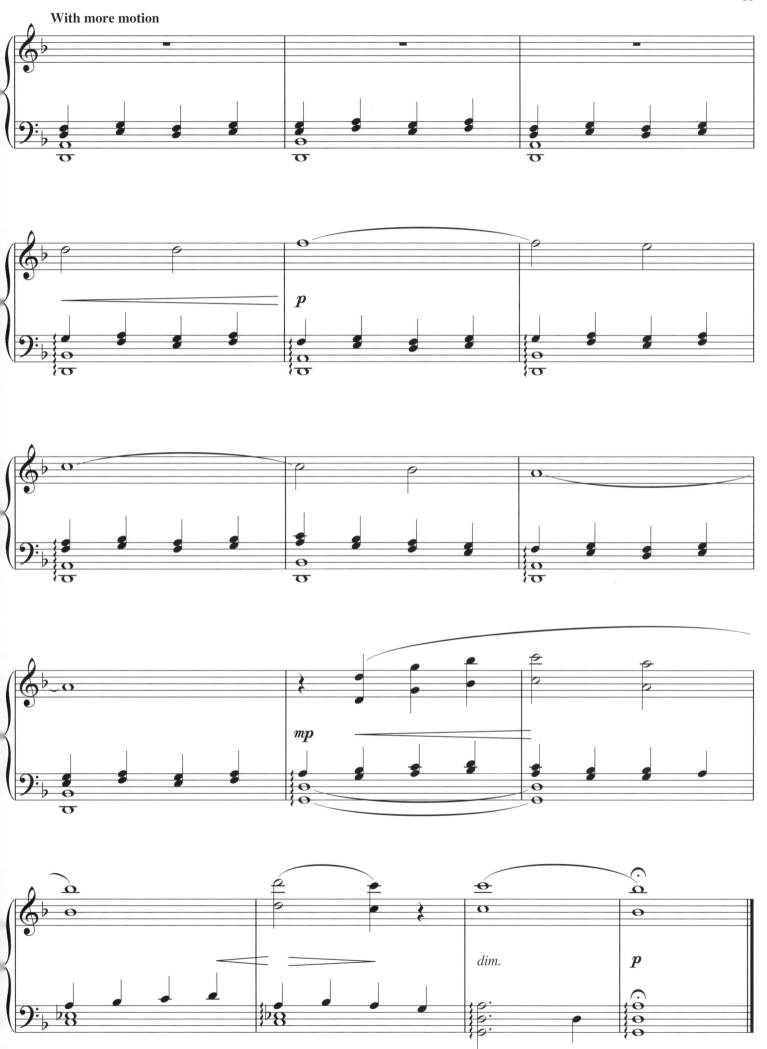

SACRIFICE

By ALEXANDRE DESPLAT

CHECK POINT

By ALEXANDRE DESPLAT

Moderately slow

With pedal

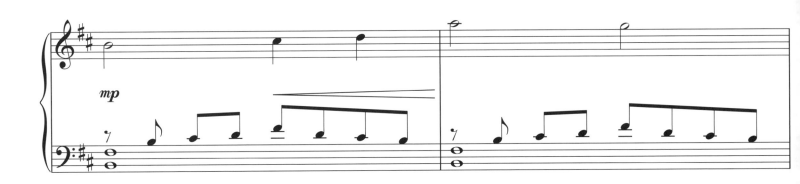

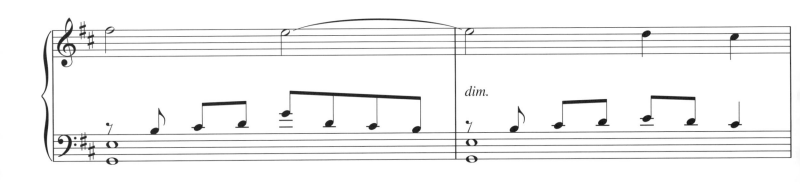

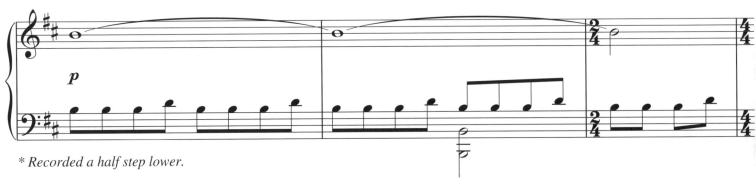

* *Recorded a half step lower.*

THE SECRET

By ALEXANDRE DESPLAT

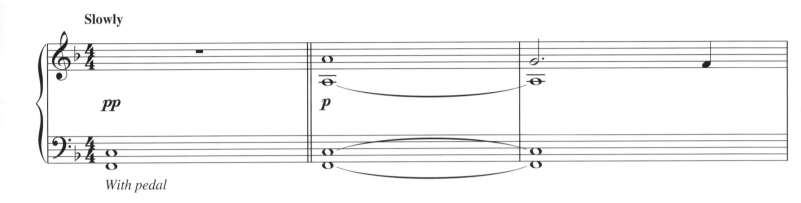

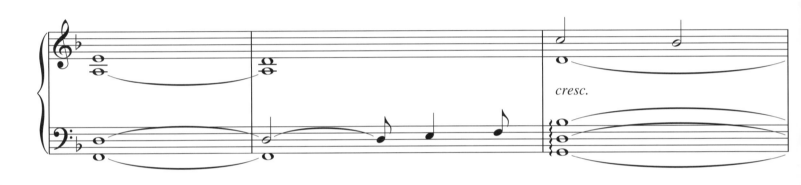

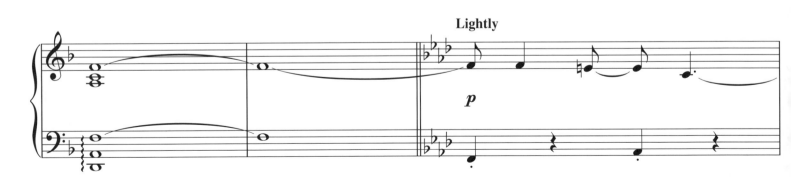

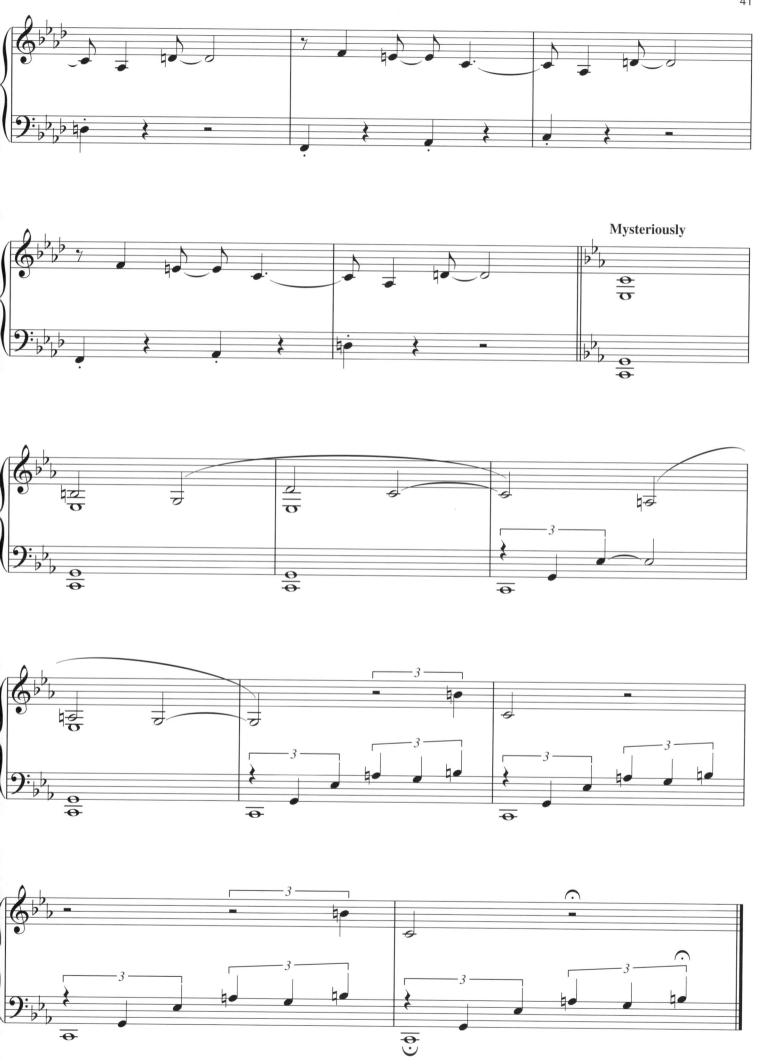

Mysteriously

REMEMBER EVERYTHING

By ALEXANDRE DESPLAT

Moderately slow

mp

With pedal

WONG CHAI CHI'S THEME

By ALEXANDRE DESPLAT

Moderately slow